J 633.79 STEW
OCT 2013
W9-CCR-020
DISCARDED

MAYBE IT'S A TYPO.

Norfolk Public Library
139 Main Street
Norfolk, MA 02056

Chocolate chip cookies.
Chocolate ice cream.
Moist, fudgy brownies.
What makes all these desserts so delicious?
Chocolate, of course.
But you can't make chocolate without . . .

THIS BOOK IS MAKING ME HUNGRY. I NEED A SNACK.
HEY, YOU'LL SPOIL YOUR DINNER.
MIND YOUR OWN BOOKWORM BUSINESS.
CHOCOLATE

. . . cocoa beans.

Cocoa beans are the seeds of the cocoa tree. Cocoa trees grow naturally in the tropical rain forests of Central and South America. But today farmers grow them in other tropical areas, too.

To make chocolate, workers spread cocoa beans with rakes and dry them in the sun. Then they roast them in a giant oven. Later, machines smash the beans into a thick paste and squeeze out the liquid to make cocoa powder. It gets mixed with a variety of ingredients to make different kinds of chocolate.

THERE'S A BUNCH OF BEANS IN THIS CHOCOLATE BAR? THAT'S RIDICULOUS.
IT'S TRUE. I READ ABOUT IT IN ANOTHER BOOK.
YOU'RE SUCH A BOOKWORM.
IT TAKES ONE TO KNOW ONE.

Cocoa beans can't develop without cocoa pods.

Cocoa pods are the fruits of the cocoa tree. They look like small, lumpy footballs growing on the tree's trunk and main branches. Inside each pod, white, gooey pulp surrounds thirty to forty cocoa beans—just enough for one candy bar.

IS A COCOA POD LIKE AN IPOD?
VERY FUNNY. NO, IT'S MORE LIKE A PEA POD.

Cocoa pods can't form without cocoa flowers . . .

When pollen from one cocoa flower lands on another cocoa flower, a tiny tube opens up inside the blossom. Pollen travels down the tube. As soon as material inside the pollen combines with material deep inside the flower, a new cocoa pod begins to grow with seeds inside.

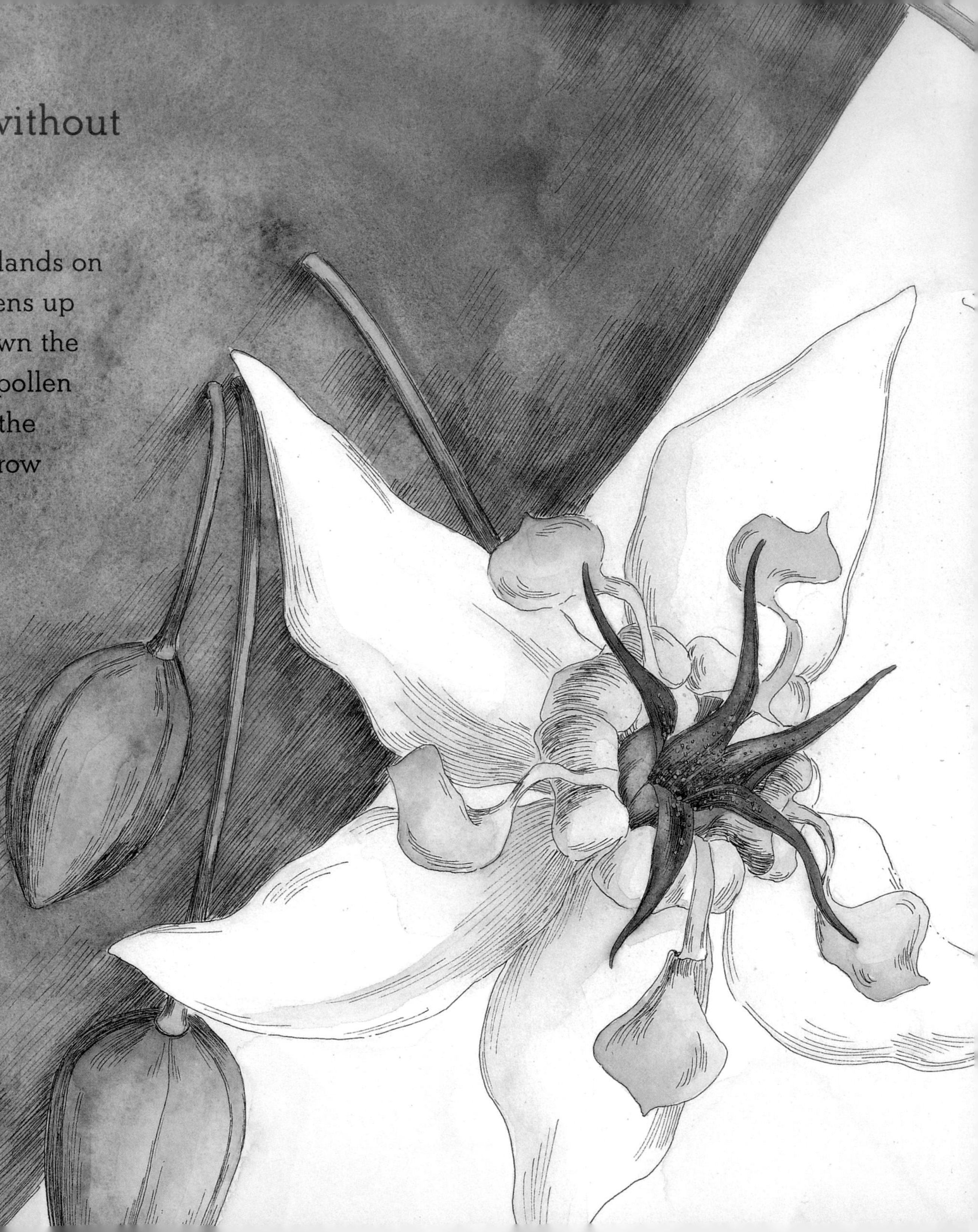

THAT'S WHAT HAPPENS INSIDE A FLOWER? PLANTS ARE AMAZING!
YOU CAN SAY THAT AGAIN!
PLANTS ARE AMAZING!

. . . and midges.

Before a female midge can lay her eggs, the little insect needs a hearty meal of rich, nutritious cocoa pollen. To find food, she crawls deep inside a cocoa blossom. As the midge climbs out, pollen sticks to her body.

When she lands on another cocoa flower, some of the pollen falls off and lands inside the blossom.

SO THAT'S HOW COCOA FLOWERS GET THE POLLEN THEY NEED TO MAKE PODS AND SEEDS.
NO MIDGES, NO CHOCOLATE.
YUP, NO MIDGES, NO CHOCOLATE.
HEY, IS THERE AN ECHO IN HERE?

Cocoa flowers can't bloom without cocoa leaves . . .

As the cocoa leaves soak up sunlight, they make sugar. The sugar travels through veins in each leaf to the tree's branches.

Then sugary sap flows through the trunk to the rest of the tree. That's how a tree gets the energy it needs to live and grow and make flowers.

I THOUGHT THIS BOOK WAS SUPPOSED TO BE ABOUT MONKEYS.
WELL, WE AREN'T DONE YET. THEY MUST BE COMING.

. . . and maggots.

As soon as leaf-cutter ants spot tender, new leaves on a cocoa tree, the little insects race to reach them.

While the hardworking ants slice up the leaves and carry the pieces back to their nest, female coffin flies land on the ants and lay eggs inside their heads.

When the eggs hatch, tiny maggots wriggle out and eat the ants' brains.

BRAIN-EATING MAGGOTS? THAT'S DISGUSTING!
MAYBE, BUT I'M GLAD THEIR MOMS LAY EGGS INSIDE THE ANTS THAT DESTROY COCOA LEAVES.
NO COFFIN FLIES, NO CHOCOLATE.

Cocoa leaves can't survive without cocoa stems . . .

A cocoa tree's trunk is a thick central stem made of wood. Its branches are smaller woody stems. The tree's smallest stems connect leaves to branches.

All these stems transport minerals and water from the tree's roots to its leaves. The leaves need the minerals to grow. They use the water to make sugary food for the whole tree.

MON-KEYS! I WANT MON-KEYS!
SHHH! I TOLD YOU NOT TO EAT THAT CHOCOLATE BAR. IT'S MAKING YOU HYPER.

. . . and lizards.

Aphids are little insects that jab holes in a cocoa tree's soft, green stems and suck up the sugary juices inside. But a hungry anole is nearby. The little lizard skitters along the tree's branches, eating aphids and other insects.

WOW! NO LIZARDS, NO CHOCOLATE.
THAT'S RIGHT. THEY EAT THE INSECTS THAT HARM COCOA STEMS.
MAYBE WE SHOULD SEND THEM A THANK-YOU NOTE.

Cocoa stems can't grow without cocoa roots . . .

A cocoa tree's roots suck up water from the soil. They also absorb minerals such as calcium and iron. The stems and the rest of the tree need these materials to live and grow. Roots also hold the cocoa tree in place.

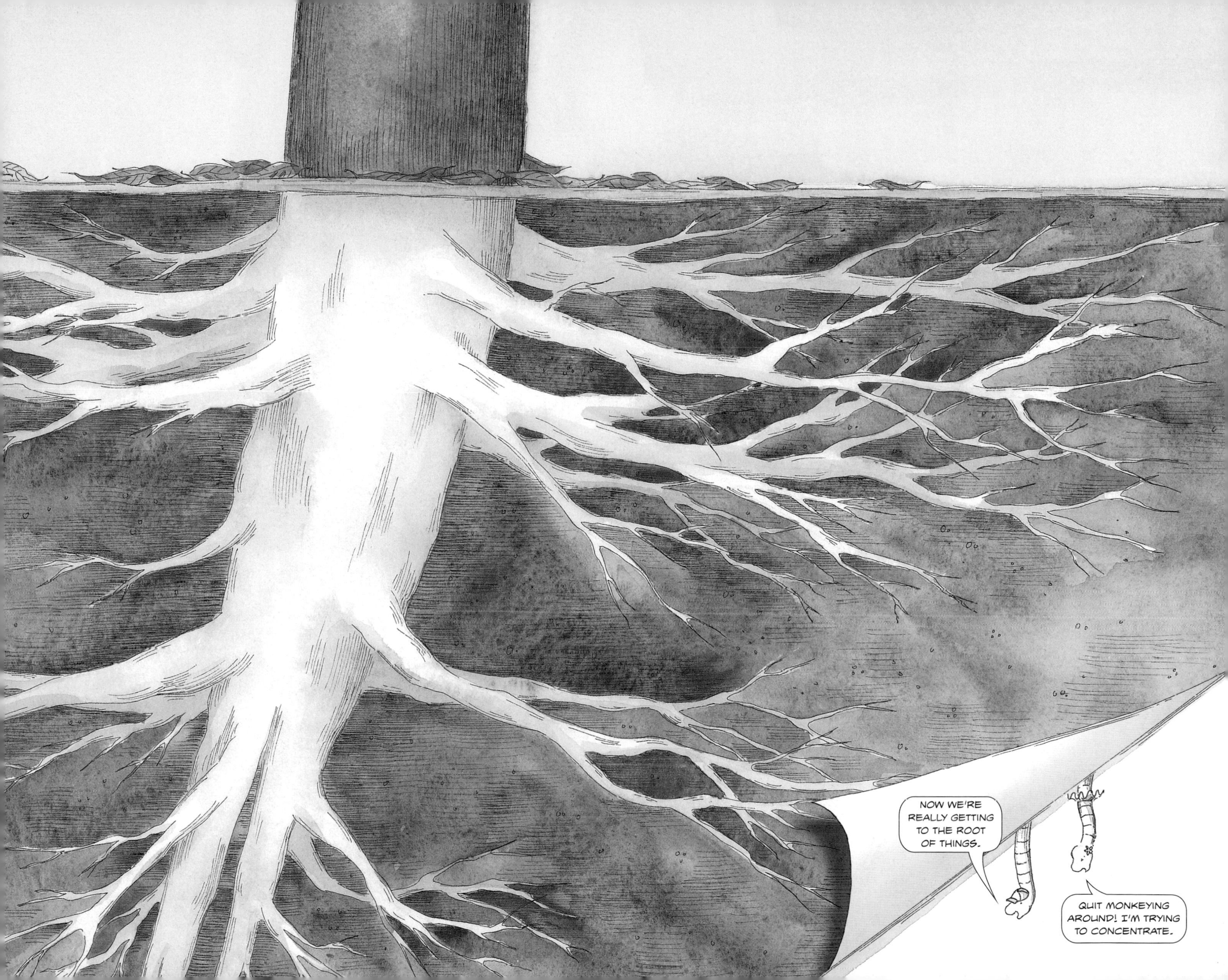
NOW WE'RE REALLY GETTING TO THE ROOT OF THINGS.
QUIT MONKEYING AROUND! I'M TRYING TO CONCENTRATE.

. . . and fungi.

Fungi live in rain forest soil. As they grow, tiny root-like threads called hyphae spread out in every direction.

When hyphae bump into a dead plant or animal, they release chemicals that break it down. Then they absorb the rotting bits and digest the minerals the fungus needs to live and grow.

The extra minerals pass out of the hyphae into the soil, where they can be absorbed by the roots of nearby cocoa trees.

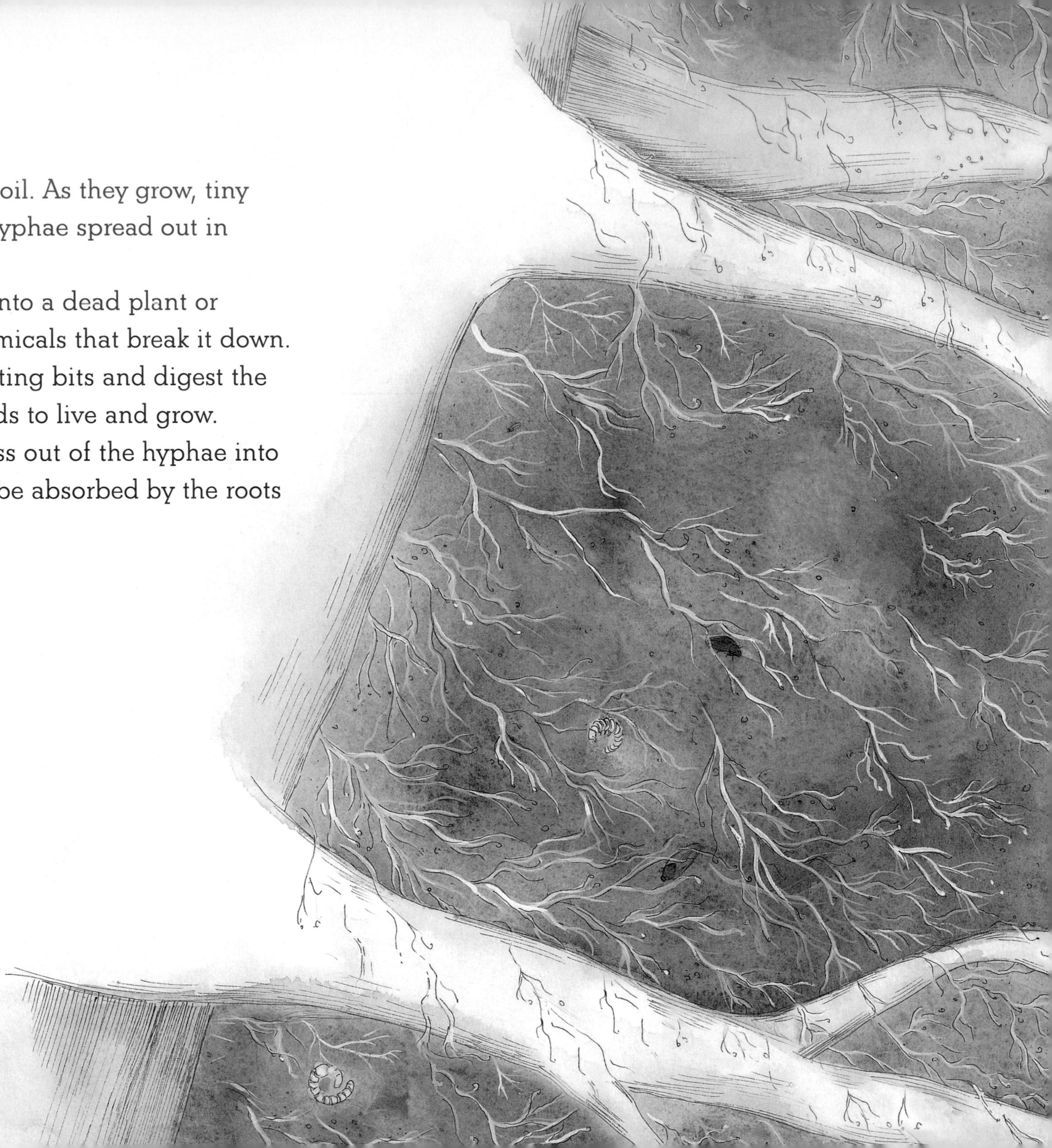

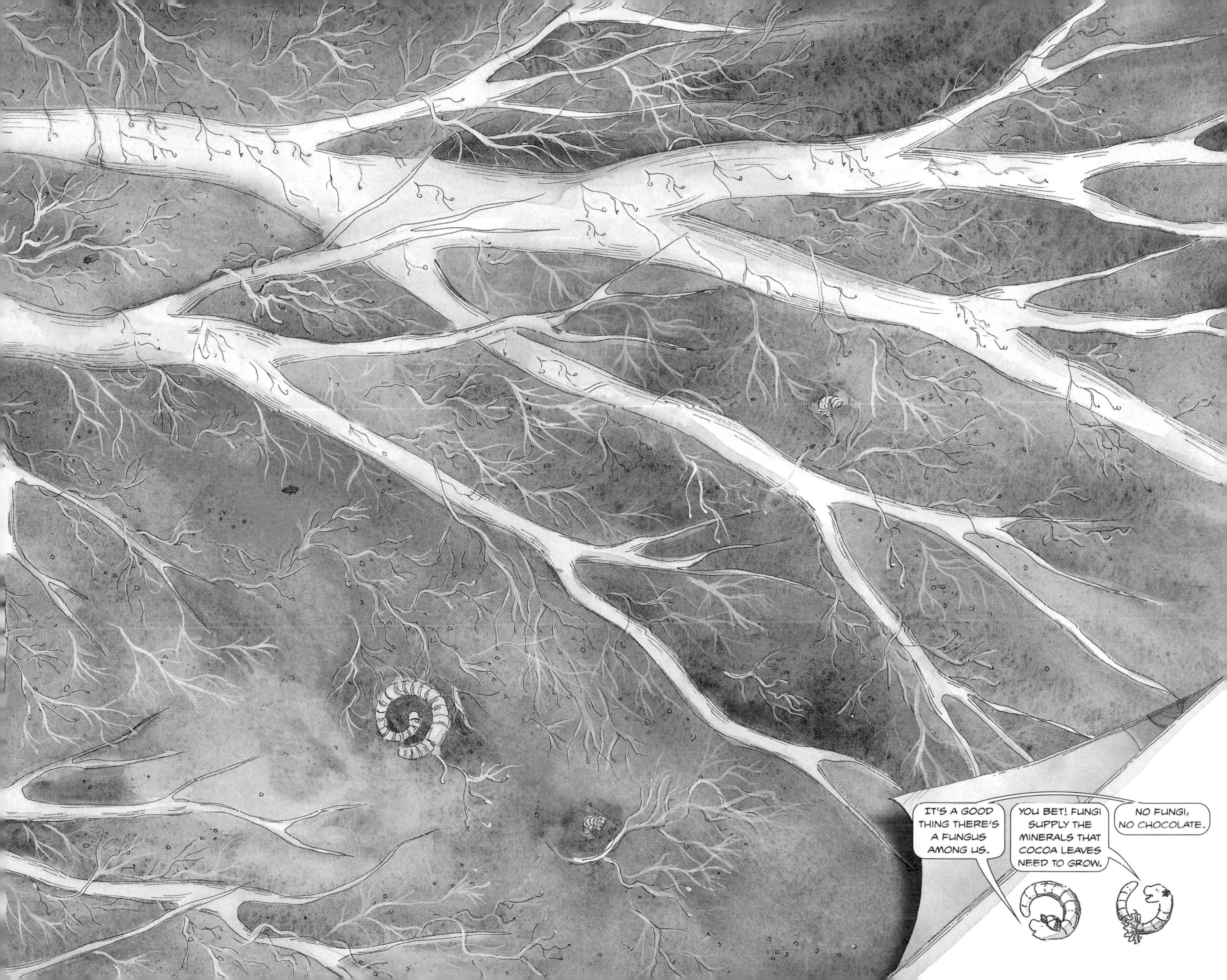
IT'S A GOOD THING THERE'S A FUNGUS AMONG US.
YOU BET! FUNGI SUPPLY THE MINERALS THAT COCOA LEAVES NEED TO GROW.
NO FUNGI, NO CHOCOLATE.

Cocoa pods, flowers, leaves, stems, and roots can't grow without cocoa beans . . .

If a cocoa bean lands in just the right place, a tiny root pushes down into the soil. Then a slender shoot stretches up toward the sky.

As time passes, the little seedling grows into a tree. When it's about five years old, the cocoa tree begins producing flowers and fruit. Some cocoa trees live up to sixty years.

WAIT A MINUTE—I THOUGHT COCOA BEANS WERE USED TO MAKE CHOCOLATE.
NOT ALL OF THEM. THERE ARE STILL PLENTY LEFT TO GROW NEW TREES.
WHAT A TREEEET! GET IT? TREE. TREAT.
THAT'S SO FUNNY I FORGOT TO LAUGH.

. . . and monkeys!

Monkeys yank pods off cocoa trees, gnaw holes in the fruits, and pull out the sticky insides. As the monkeys travel through the rain forest, they suck on the lemony-lime pulp and spit out the beans.

Cocoa pods never fall off cocoa trees. If monkeys and a few other animals didn't scatter cocoa beans on the ground, new cocoa trees couldn't grow.

AT LAST, THE MONKEYS! NOW THAT CRAZY TITLE ACTUALLY MAKES SENSE.
THAT'S RIGHT. NO MONKEYS, NO CHOCOLATE. THE SEEDS MONKEYS SPIT OUT END UP GROWING INTO NEW TREES.

Cocoa and Rain Forests

On traditional cocoa farms, workers plant cocoa trees in neat rows with only a few kinds of trees shading them from the sun. Under these conditions fewer than five percent of all cocoa flowers produce pods.

Recently scientists discovered that cocoa trees produce more pods when they grow in patches of thinned-out rain forest, where many other kinds of trees provide shade. These cocoa groves are the perfect home for the midges that pollinate cocoa and the coffin-fly maggots that attack leaf-cutter ants. They're also great places for lizards, monkeys, and other rain-forest creatures to find food.

Hopefully more cocoa farmers will begin growing trees in rain-forest cocoa groves. In the last thirty years, more than forty percent of the world's tropical rain forests have been destroyed. And right now we're losing one hundred acres every minute. At that rate rain forests could be gone in fifty years. Cocoa groves can do more than provide us with a steady supply of cocoa beans. They can also give many different species of rain-forest plants and animals places to live.

What You Can Do to Help

1. Read more books about tropical rain forests and the creatures that live in them. Then share what you've learned with your family and friends.
2. Join a group that helps protect rain forests.
3. Work with people at your school to raise money for organizations that buy and preserve tropical rain-forest land.
4. Live in a way that decreases your impact on the natural world:
    - Turn off lights and computers when you leave a room.
    - In the winter, put on a sweater and keep your house a little cooler.
    - In the summer, use air conditioning only when necessary.
    - Take shorter showers, and turn off the water while you brush your teeth.
    - If you buy a new computer or TV, look for energy-efficient products.
    - Encourage your parents to bring reusable bags to the grocery store.
    - Eat less meat and more locally grown fruits and vegetables.
    - Recycle bottles, cans, and paper at home and at school.
    - Compost your food waste and use it to fertilize a garden.
    - Plant a tree in your yard or at your school.

I DON'T THINK MONKEYS SHOULD GET ALL THE GLORY. WHY AREN'T COFFIN FLIES, LIZARDS, AND FUNGI IN THE TITLE, TOO?

YOU'RE RIGHT. THEY'RE ALL IMPORTANT. SO ARE THE TROPICAL RAIN FORESTS WHERE THEY ALL LIVE.

Author's Note

During an afternoon walk in 2003, I literally stopped to smell the roses and was startled by what I saw—aphids sucking sap, ladybugs devouring the aphids, ants battling the ladybugs. The thriving, active microhabitat inspired me to write, but I knew I needed to focus on a more appealing plant.

I found that plant—the cocoa tree—during a 2005 trip to Costa Rica. I scoured the scientific literature to discover what pollinates cocoa, what disperses its seeds, and what attacks its foliage. But I came up empty. At last I tracked down Allen Young, the world's leading expert on cocoa-tree pollination and growth. He had all the information I needed and agreed to be my co-author. That's when the work really began.

I wrote and revised, wrote and revised, trying many different story structures. I kept asking myself, "What's the most engaging way to convey this information?" By 2008 I knew the book would feature layered text with a "House That Jack Built" feel, but I still needed a way to reinforce the book's complex ideas without being didactic.

The solution came while discussing Halloween costumes with my nieces. I said that their dad's best childhood costume was the Swedish Chef from *The Muppet Show*. Did they want to be Kermit and Miss Piggy? No. How about Statler and Waldorf, the two old guys in the balcony? As they giggled, something clicked in my mind. That's what my book needed—characters to comment on the text and add humor. But not old guys. It needed bookworms! With the final piece in place, *No Monkeys, No Chocolate* was born.

For Caroline, my chocolate-loving little monkey
—M. S.

For beautiful Morpho, a large dazzling blue butterfly alighting on a fermenting cocoa bean to imbibe its sweet juices, awash in a cocoon of humidity on the forest floor
—A. Y.

To my favorite chocolate lover, Dan
—N. W.

Text copyright © 2013 by Melissa Stewart and Allen Young
Illustrations copyright © 2013 by Nicole Wong
All rights reserved, including the right of reproduction in whole or in part in any form.
Charlesbridge and colophon are registered trademarks of Charlesbridge Publishing, Inc.

Published by Charlesbridge
85 Main Street
Watertown, MA 02472
(617) 926-0329
www.charlesbridge.com

Library of Congress Cataloging-in-Publication Data
Stewart, Melissa.
No monkeys, no chocolate / Melissa Stewart and Allen Young; illustrated by Nicole Wong.
p. cm.
ISBN 978-1-58089-287-2 (reinforced for library use)
ISBN 978-1-60734-609-8 (ebook)
1. Cacao—Juvenile literature. 2. Cacao beans—Juvenile literature. 3. Cacao—Diseases and pests—Juvenile literature. 4. Cocoa processing—Juvenile literature. 5. Chocolate—Juvenile literature. I. Young, Allen M. II. Wong, Nicole (Nicole E.), ill. III. Title.

SB267.S67 2013
633.7'4–dc23 2012000789

Printed in Singapore
(hc) 10 9 8 7 6 5 4 3 2 1

Illustrations done in ink and watercolor on Fabriano watercolor paper
Display type set in Chaloops by The Chank Company
Text type set in Beton and Blambot Classic by Nate Piekos, Blambot.com
Color separations by Chroma Graphics, Singapore
Printed and bound February 2013 by Imago in Singapore
Production supervision by Brian G. Walker
Designed by Diane M. Earley

HOW ABOUT A STANDING O FOR THE ENTIRE COCOA-BEAN TEAM?
UM, WE DON'T HAVE HANDS OR FEET.
NOT THAT KIND OF STANDING O. THIS KIND.

Norfolk Public Library
139 Main Street
Norfolk, MA 02056